# This camping journal belongs to

_____

 # My Camping Trip

| Where | When | With who |
|---|---|---|
|  |  |  |

### Favorite things I did- draw or write!

Draw an animal you saw

My campsite

# More about my camping adventure
## Add stickers, draw, write

---

# Scavenger Hunt
## Put an X on the box when you find these objects

# My Camping Trip

| Where | When | With who |
|---|---|---|
|  |  |  |

### Favorite things I did- draw or write!

Draw an animal you saw

My campsite

# More about my camping adventure
Add stickers, draw, write

---

# Scavenger Hunt
Put an X on the box when you find these objects

 # My Camping Trip

| Where | When | With who |
|-------|------|----------|
|       |      |          |

**Favorite things I did- draw or write!**

Draw an animal you saw

My campsite

# More about my camping adventure
## Add stickers, draw, write

---

# Scavenger Hunt
### Put an X on the box when you find these objects

 # My Camping Trip

| Where | When | With who |
|-------|------|----------|
|       |      |          |

### Favorite things I did- draw or write!

Draw an animal you saw

My campsite

# More about my camping adventure
## Add stickers, draw, write

---

# Scavenger Hunt
Put an X on the box when you find these objects

 # My Camping Trip

| Where | When | With who |
|:---:|:---:|:---:|
| | | |

### Favorite things I did- draw or write!

Draw an animal you saw

My campsite

# More about my camping adventure
## Add stickers, draw, write

---

# Scavenger Hunt
Put an X on the box when you find these objects

 # My Camping Trip

**Where**

**When**

**With who**

Favorite things I did- draw or write!

Draw an animal you saw

My campsite

# More about my camping adventure
## Add stickers, draw, write

---

# Scavenger Hunt
Put an X on the box when you find these objects

# My Camping Trip

**Where**

**When**

**With who**

Favorite things I did- draw or write!

Draw an animal you saw

My campsite

# More about my camping adventure
### Add stickers, draw, write

---

# Scavenger Hunt
Put an X on the box when you find these objects

 # My Camping Trip

| Where | When | With who |
|---|---|---|
| | | |

### Favorite things I did- draw or write!

Draw an animal you saw

My campsite

# More about my camping adventure
### Add stickers, draw, write

---

## Scavenger Hunt
### Put an X on the box when you find these objects

# My Camping Trip

**Where**

**When**

**With who**

Favorite things I did- draw or write!

Draw an animal you saw

My campsite

# More about my camping adventure
Add stickers, draw, write

---

# Scavenger Hunt
Put an X on the box when you find these objects

 # My Camping Trip

**Where**

**When**

**With who**

Favorite things I did- draw or write!

Draw an animal you saw

My campsite

# More about my camping adventure
Add stickers, draw, write

---

# Scavenger Hunt
Put an X on the box when you find these objects

# My Camping Trip

**Where**

**When**

**With who**

Favorite things I did- draw or write!

Draw an animal you saw

My campsite

# More about my camping adventure
Add stickers, draw, write

---

## Scavenger Hunt
Put an X on the box when you find these objects

 # My Camping Trip

**Where**

**When**

**With who**

Favorite things I did- draw or write!

Draw an animal you saw

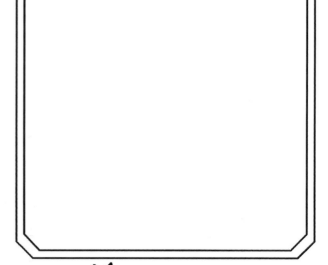

My campsite

# More about my camping adventure
### Add stickers, draw, write

---

# Scavenger Hunt
### Put an X on the box when you find these objects

 # My Camping Trip

**Where**

**When**

**With who**

Favorite things I did- draw or write!

Draw an animal you saw

My campsite

# More about my camping adventure
Add stickers, draw, write

---

# Scavenger Hunt
Put an X on the box when you find these objects

 # My Camping Trip

**Where**

**When**

**With who**

### Favorite things I did- draw or write!

Draw an animal you saw

My campsite

# More about my camping adventure
### Add stickers, draw, write

---

# Scavenger Hunt
### Put an X on the box when you find these objects

 # My Camping Trip

| Where | When | With who |
|:-----:|:----:|:--------:|
|       |      |          |

### Favorite things I did- draw or write!

Draw an animal you saw          My campsite

# More about my camping adventure
Add stickers, draw, write

---

# Scavenger Hunt
Put an X on the box when you find these objects

 # My Camping Trip

**Where**

**When**

**With who**

## Favorite things I did- draw or write!

Draw an animal you saw

My campsite

# More about my camping adventure
Add stickers, draw, write

---

# Scavenger Hunt
Put an X on the box when you find these objects

# My Camping Trip

| Where | When | With who |
|-------|------|----------|
|       |      |          |

Favorite things I did- draw or write!

Draw an animal you saw

My campsite

# More about my camping adventure
Add stickers, draw, write

---

# Scavenger Hunt
Put an X on the box when you find these objects

# My Camping Trip

**Where**

**When**

**With who**

Favorite things I did- draw or write!

Draw an animal you saw

My campsite

# More about my camping adventure
## Add stickers, draw, write

---

# Scavenger Hunt
## Put an X on the box when you find these objects

# My Camping Trip

| Where | When | With who |
|---|---|---|
|  |  |  |

Favorite things I did- draw or write!

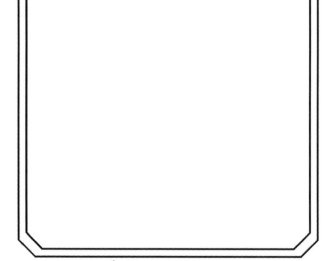

Draw an animal you saw

My campsite

# More about my camping adventure
Add stickers, draw, write

---

# Scavenger Hunt
Put an X on the box when you find these objects

# My Camping Trip

**Where**

**When**

**With who**

Favorite things I did- draw or write!

Draw an animal you saw

My campsite

# More about my camping adventure
## Add stickers, draw, write

---

# Scavenger Hunt
## Put an X on the box when you find these objects

 # My Camping Trip

| Where | When | With who |
|---|---|---|
|  |  |  |

**Favorite things I did- draw or write!**

Draw an animal you saw  My campsite

# More about my camping adventure
Add stickers, draw, write

---

# Scavenger Hunt
Put an X on the box when you find these objects

 # My Camping Trip

**Where**

**When**

**With who**

Favorite things I did- draw or write!

Draw an animal you saw

My campsite

# More about my camping adventure
### Add stickers, draw, write

---

# Scavenger Hunt
### Put an X on the box when you find these objects

# My Camping Trip

**Where**

**When**

**With who**

Favorite things I did- draw or write!

Draw an animal you saw

My campsite

# More about my camping adventure
### Add stickers, draw, write

---

## Scavenger Hunt
### Put an X on the box when you find these objects

# My Camping Trip

Where

When

With who

Favorite things I did- draw or write!

Draw an animal you saw

My campsite

# More about my camping adventure
Add stickers, draw, write

---

# Scavenger Hunt
Put an X on the box when you find these objects

# My Camping Trip

| Where | When | With who |
|-------|------|----------|
|       |      |          |

## Favorite things I did- draw or write!

Draw an animal you saw

My campsite

# More about my camping adventure
### Add stickers, draw, write

---

# Scavenger Hunt
### Put an X on the box when you find these objects

 # My Camping Trip

**Where**

**When**

**With who**

Favorite things I did- draw or write!

Draw an animal you saw

My campsite

# More about my camping adventure
### Add stickers, draw, write

---

# Scavenger Hunt
### Put an X on the box when you find these objects

 # My Camping Trip

**Where**

**When**

**With who**

Favorite things I did- draw or write!

Draw an animal you saw

My campsite

# More about my camping adventure
## Add stickers, draw, write

---

# Scavenger Hunt
### Put an X on the box when you find these objects

# My Camping Trip

**Where**

**When**

**With who**

**Favorite things I did- draw or write!**

Draw an animal you saw

My campsite

# More about my camping adventure
Add stickers, draw, write

---

# Scavenger Hunt
Put an X on the box when you find these objects

# My Camping Trip

| Where | When | With who |
|---|---|---|
| | | |

**Favorite things I did- draw or write!**

Draw an animal you saw

My campsite

# More about my camping adventure
Add stickers, draw, write

---

# Scavenger Hunt
Put an X on the box when you find these objects

# Fun camping activity ideas

Play flashlight tag
Play Tic Tac Toe in the dirt
Paint Rocks
Imitate bird calls
Collect nature items (rocks, sticks, pine cones)
Make something with the nature items
Decorate your own walking stick
Go stargazing
Swimming

Add your own fun activities

# Camping Bingo

| | | | | |
|---|---|---|---|---|
| mushroom | worm | flat rock | ★ | camp store |
| tent | insect | black rock | V shaped branch | bike |
| tree stump | ★ | bird | acorn | dog |
| pinecone | s'more | tree moss | ★ | feather |
| sleeping bag | flower | firewood | spider web | bee |

# Other camping memories

# Other camping memories

# Other camping memories

# Other camping memories

# Other camping memories

# Other camping memories

# Other camping memories

# Other camping memories

Made in the USA
Coppell, TX
09 December 2021

67494619R00039